IN THESE DAYS AND NIGHTS:

A UNIVERSAL PEACE EVOCATION

FOR EACH MONTH OF THE YEAR

Dwight Russel Micnhimer
Minister, Universal Life Church

Copyright © 2016 D. Russel Micnhimer

All rights reserved.

ISBN 978-1523292110

First Edition 09 08 07 06 05 04 03 02 01

Photography by the author

Typesetting Nalini Priyadarshni

DEDICATION

In loving memory
of my Mother and Father
Dwight B and Carolyn F. Micnhimer

Foreword

Only when individuals are at Peace may the world be at Peace. This collection of evocations reminds readers of the ways and practices whereby they may find that peace. It is arranged conveniently into twelve parts that correspond to the months of the year. Accompanying each is a series of images that lend themselves to contemplation and meditation. Bringing individual meaning to universal images allows the merger of personal knowings with universal.

I have deliberately left the punctuation quite ill defined so that individual voices may emphasis and connect the ideas according to their own predilections and preferences. Likewise I have refrained from naming deities and attributes so that this work may be held up as a reflection no matter the background of the reader.

Universal Peace is an ideal. One that I have come to feel is obtainable through individual growth and development. I hope this thin volume will aid you in the achievement of your own steps toward that goal.

Hunger is a universal need that interrupts the movement toward peace in many ways. There is no simple answer to that problem. But on an individual level we can do something about it by feeding one mouth at a time. All royalties paid the author from the sale of this book will be gifted to local food banks without any processing fees deducted. If you are part of a group seeking ways to contribute to the alleviation of hunger in your community, you might want to consider the resale of this devotional toward that end.

Dwight Russel Micnhimer, Oregon, USA January 2016

"Do only that which is right"

J

January

In these days of nights of our living

May the goodness of the universe

Be attracted to our devotions

And words of our reverent song

Be reflected with great magnitude

May the reflections and reverberations

Of our holy intent

Reach micro and macrocosm

To fullest extent

May it be our gracious fortune

To share complete content

May our knowing of the bounty

Of universal essence

Give us cause for eternal thanks

May our endeavors be guided

By beneficent higher forces

And lead us to clear visions

Of our future that leads to our success

May we rejoice in our days

And the bounty that nourishes us

Honoring all ways and always

The source from which it flows

May we share the blessing we

Received from the diligence of our work

With those who are of need around us

May our hearts beat ever joyous

In tune with the songs we are destined

To sing and may its harmonies

Mark well the moments of our passing

Please bless each breath we take

In harmony with the divine

FEBRUARY

In these days and nights of our loving

May the wisdom of eternity

Smile on each breath of our knowing

May the strength of all our learnings

Caress the weariness from our bones

So we may persevere in the

Reflection of the will that is our way

May we learn to obey the guidance

That arrives so freely given

May our eternal care in thought

And deed lead us to honor

All that we hold dear. May the nearness

Of our knowing lead to perpetual growth

Brighten as reflection of our

Truest honesty that whole is one

And one is whole and one and one

Is one and whole and whole is whole

May our correspondences lead us always

Through the bright lights of understanding

Our differences are what make

Us complete. May our assimilation

Of differences help us heal and

Dwell in the strength that is our heritage

From all those hearts that beat before;

May the beats of our heart honor

All those who beat before by their

Remembrance. Let us always know

The true heartbeat of our nature is

Always with us.

MARCH

In these days and nights of our loving

Let us concentrate the power of life

By honoring it in each living – Living

Each moment to its fullest

May we enhance the collective

Great bloom of its becoming and

Celebrate with each movement its

Unique universal expression

May the peace of all peace fill

Our rest with renewal so

That we may abide in the strength of

Our rejuvenation and lift our arms

And legs tirelessly in reflection and

Celebration of the beauty that enhances the

Glory of our tribulations in this

Space and time. May the face of

Time and the spice of space enhance

Our pleasures in the growing

Of our grace in the heart of love.

May we be granted excellent tools of our trade

And teachings of our trade; may their

Worth increase and honor the sweat

Of its founders as we give thanks

For the lessons they so skillfully crafted

And passed along. May the receptors

Of our hearts be always and all ways

Open to the skills that fill the

Dimples of the smiles in which we triumph

Over our travails. May our travails

Be trivial compared

To our triumphs

APRIL

In the days and nights of our living

May our renewals be our legacy, testimony

That we have heard the growings

On this earth of the powers below it

And the powers above it, and the powers

That flow through it, and the powers

Which know it. May we awaken

To each breath of knowing

That we embody and allow it

To shine through the whole of

All our parts. May we recognize

Our compliments in the faces of the

Smiles that we meet, may our

Gait be level in the balance

Of up and down, may our views

Be broad and our focus narrow

May the mercies of our fate

Accumulate into a bouquet divine

In which each part of the whole

Answers each question as it occurs;

May answers to our confusions

Be timely in their becoming

May the proper forces of our clime

Bless us with their timely manifestations

And the ebbs and flows of the tides

Of the sea on which we ride be kind

And guides us to shores of peace

MAY

In these days and nights of our living

May the shoots of our ambitions

Spring forth from our fertile seed

May thanks to the forces that

Bind us to their strength be the tribute

We offer to their longevity

May the chance interception

Of adverse fate in our path

Not deter us from the promise

Of our purpose. Grant us if it

Be in accord with universal will

The patience to understand the convolutions

That lead us to our greatest understanding

Of our goings and of our standings still

May each trying of our understanding

Lead to greater patience and greater

Diligence to be receptive to knowing

May the rest that is part of the fruit

Of our labor be adequate and savory

May joy fill the moments of our stillness

And in those moments may we renew

Our connection with the calm joy of infinity

May our unfoldings leave our views

Exposed to awakening from each source

Far and near, that leads and guides us

Towards their revelation of our total self

As embodied in the universal spirit

Humble us before the powers that flow through us

And translate and transform our actions and our words

May we reawaken each day in safe warm

Light, may we shine each hour

Until our journey is complete

JUNE

In these days and nights of our living

May we honor our beginnings and

Those who made it so; may we

Honor those from those we have learned

By living the lessons they have taught.

May our hearts be glad with each wisdom

Gained no matter what the lesson cost.

May we be part of a whole without

Boundaries; may the boundaries of our parts

Make us whole. May the joy of true love

Be the guiding stream that carries us

To the shores of ecstasy; may we always

Remember the boats that brought us there; may

We leave them behind for others to share

On the beach; may our footsteps be firm

Across emotion's dunes; may we raise

A joyous song of praise for the Maker,

Of praise for the Shaker, of praise for the

Taker, of praise for the Power that Preserves. May we always

Remember to give thanks for our provision

And thanks for the strength that provides

The visions that turn our will into action

And our actions into reflections that honor

Our sources. May each beam ridge in our roof

Be strong and protect us from the elements;

To manifest a bright reflection of their purpose.

May our purpose be in accordance with the Will

That shines like a beacon to all

From deep within our Heart

JULY

In these days and nights of our living

May we celebrate the joy of each moment

And its connection with the whole

May the sparkles in the trails of the

Fireworks we are be replicas of the infinite

Spark that animates us all. Let each

Of our smiles be the afterglow of

The great light that creates

Each syllable of sound we utter

May we be ever vigilant of the freedoms

Our forefathers and mothers sought

To guarantee, may we be ever vigilant

In the level of our acceptance of tyranny

May the revolutions of our understanding

Lead revolt against all that represses

The clear tones bursting from our heart

May we always be for the peace

Rather than against the war, may

Our communication be mutual and

Creative and mutually creative; may

Each blending of our experiences lead

To wisest wisdom until there is only

Wisdom and all its variations are one.

May our fondest desires be granted by

The value of the wisdom of our ways

May memory persist until the heart

Of time is a single beat with our own and

In the beat of that each moment may the

Smile on the face of the infinite dispel

Every frown that disapproves from the retina

That focuses the field of our vision on the

Heartbeat of our dreams

AUGUST

In these days and nights of our living

May the unfailing mantra of our

Conventions embody efficiency to

Enhance effort that leads towards perfection

May we reflect and reflect upon the

Harvest of our strivings, may our

Strivings lead to thrivings guided

By wisdom, action and form;

May we know the wisdom mind

Creates first hand as it creates

Clarity from chaos. May our way

Be clear before us, transparent to

Our knowing, unclouded by doubt

Uncluttered with attached debris;

May our anchors always drop in

Calm waters and there be a fish eager

For bait, may the deer and elk

Graze on sweet grass; may the plans

For the hunt take order based on the eyes

Of the hungry; may our bowstrings

Be taut. Protect our rows from

The teeth of our competition. May our

Purity of intent protect us from harm

May our arms be strong to protect

The interests of our hearts; may our

Words be gentle and loud so they

May be most widely understood

May the heartbeat that is the universe

Always and all ways beat its beat

Through us, let us sing always a

Song of glory in praise of all we

May never know but dream that we

Are drawing near

SEPTEMBER

In the days and nights of our living

May we remember to rend our thanks

To the provider whose name is beyond knowing

For each blessing that we receive

May we understand that the systole

And diastole of the sun is the bread

That provides for the power of our knowing

May we know the peace of the cycles

Within and without, may their crests

Fit gently in our valleys; may the foam

We are on the ocean make a difference

In the sculpture of the waves; may

We recognize our teachers in the students

We become; may we recognize our students

In the teachers we become. May we

Kneel in the temple of each breath,

Brightening each horizon with

The measures our hearts etch on the sea

Of our tranquility. May we be

"Shaped and fashioned by what we love"

May our love reside in the depths

Of the heart from which all love flows

May we be divine reflections of our

Connections with all that has gone before

And all that is ahead in the future

May each now be an affirmation

Of our connection to the heartbeat

Of now that is forever—a fixed

Polaris guiding even our folly

To a bonding with the beat,

The beat that goes on, the beat that

Proclaims we are members of the band

OCTOBER

In these days and night of our living

May we hold dear the teachings

Our for-bearers sought to bear;

May their faith further our understanding

And awaken to wisdom the most dormant

Of our parts; may all our parts

Be wakened to partake of the feast

That each breath affords us, no matter

What our vine; we are all connected

May we always remember to give thanks

For the rest that rest provides;

Give thanks for our pleasure and thanks

For our pain; may we learn to

Teach the triumphs over our travails.

May we share the harvest of all our endeavors;

May they reflect the purest of our knowings.

May we be protected in our comings

And our goings by our accordance

With the Tao; may we know

Our place, our face and our pace

So the smile that we wear is universal

And the scarf around our voice is hope,

The shade above our eyes is knowing.

That the measure of our becoming is doing.

May our notes and syllables of praise and asking

Be heard and understood. May our reverence

Please the Whole to whom it is offered

May our hearts be eternally strong

So that we breathe from the Power

Of the breath that breathes us:

May our every breath reflect the story

And the Glory that makes us whole.

NOVEMBER

In these days and nights of our living

May we never forget the words and songs

That led us to our understandings

May we honor the traditions

That have made us whole

Let our efforts praise that which we hold most high

Let our echoes ring from the walls

Of every care. Let our hearts

Lead many to their understanding

May we always be granted the strength

To accomplish our changes. May our hearts

know love that is the divine expressing itself through us

May our accomplishments honor always the spirit

That from within us creates; may we be receptive

To the inspiration that is our connection with

The source of all inspiration; may it be a

Perpetually renewing beacon that guides

Each stride of our breath towards the top of

The source that is perpetual, each cycle

A systole and diastole of our awakening, each

New note a symphony of the heart beats that

Have gone before into new realms of understanding

May the light of our first illuminations always return

Us to our truths and may we honor

Those early shapings of our course

May the unchanging canvas upon which

Our actions are the painting always

Reflect the unshaken brush of the artist

Whose calm hand and heart mediate our brief

Grief over our bones turning to dust

And all but our spirit passing away; that

The essences of our knowing, as sure as

They are singular, are always.

DECEMBER

In these days and nights of our living

May our goings and our comings,

Between our sleepings and our waking

Fill our hearts with joy in our celebrations

With our links to jubilation; may

The wings and songs of joy

Overtake us; may our passion

Forever bond us to the songs we sing

In celebration of the passion of the art

May the realization of unity be the goal of our diversity;

May difference and diversity be our

Common bond; may there be from

Plant Earth one strong song of birth

Birth of consciousness saying we are here

Conscious that we are one even in our diversity

Aware that we are young; aware that our

Learning has just begun. May each breath

Be adventure; each day a new thrill;

May our hearts revel all their days

Interacting with a world that is new

May we be granted patience to endure

And prolong the travails and pleasures

Of our steps. May we take each step

Reverently reflecting all we were

Designed to be, being ever thankful

For our pattern, inspired by the

Grand design; humble in our magnitude,

Shining bright in every facet. May

We always and all ways be the sharpest

Brightest reflection from each facet of

That jewel of jewels of which

There is none brighter

1

Made in the USA
Charleston, SC
31 March 2016